# WE'RE TALKING ABOUT
# DRUGS

**JENNY BRYAN**

Wayland

Editor: Catherine Baxter
Design: John Christopher
Consultant: Andrew Fraser, Drug Advice and Information Service, Brighton, East Sussex

This edition published in 1997 by Wayland Publishers Ltd

First published in 1995 by Wayland Publishers Ltd
61 Western Road, Hove, East Sussex, BN3 1JD, England

© Copyright 1995 Wayland (Publishers) Ltd.

Find Wayland on the internet at http://www.wayland.co.uk

British Library Cataloguing in Publication Data

Bryan, Jenny
We're Talking About Drugs. – 2nd ed.
1. Narcotics – Juvenile literature
2. Drug abuse – Juvenile literature
I. Title II. Drugs
362.2'9

Paperback ISBN 0 7502 2143 7

Typeset by Strong Silent Type, England
Printed and bound in Italy by G. Canale & C.S.p.A., Turin

Picture Acknowledgements

APM cover, title page, 4 (top & bottom), 5 (top & bottom), 11 (top & bottom), 12, 15, 18, 27; Impact 14 (Paul Lowe); Life File 7 (Jeremy Hoare), 8 (top, Mo Khan), 9 (Arthur Jumper); 13 (Ian Richards), 20 (Jon Woodhouse); Sally & Richard Greenhill 21, 26; Christine Osborne 22, 24; Tony Stone 10 (Jon Riley), 19 (Ken Whitmore), 23 (André Szramko); Topham 6; Rex Features 16 (top & bottom), 17 (top & bottom), 19, 28, 29; Science Photo Library 25 (Michael Abbey).

All of the children who are featured in this book are models.

# Contents

Go on, try some! — 4
How drugs affect your body — 6
Where do drugs come from? — 8
But my parents smoke and drink… — 10
Adam's story — 12
Emma's story — 14
Wasted lives — 16
Richard's story — 18
Uppers and downers — 20
Drugs and crime — 22
Drugs and disease — 24
Andy's story — 26
Getting help — 28

Glossary — 30
Further reading — 31
Index — 32

# Go on, try some!

Yesterday, Adam's best friend Kevin offered him a joint. They had left school early and gone home to Kevin's house while his parents were at work. They had done it before and they usually smoked a few cigarettes. Adam was surprised when Kevin suggested they smoke some cannabis that he'd found in his Mum's cupboard. He made an excuse and went home but he's sure Kevin will offer him drugs again and isn't sure what to do.

▲ Adam was offered a joint.

Emma is going to her first rave party on Saturday. She's really glad to have been asked because all her friends are going. But one of them is going to take some Ecstasy to the party and Emma's worried about looking silly if she turns it down.

◀ Emma's going to a rave party.

John is very worried about his older brother, Richard. He uses cocaine. He says he can give it up any time he wants but John doesn't think he can and doesn't know what to do.

Andy sniffs glue. He's been doing it for two years and wishes he could stop. Sometimes it makes him sick and it gives him headaches. Last week a neighbour caught him with a bag over his face in the shopping precinct and Andy is scared about what will happen to him.

▲ John is worried about his older brother, Richard.

Adam, Emma, John and Andy have all heard about the dangers of drugs. But what should they do? Should Adam avoid his friend Kevin? Should Emma stay home on Saturday? Should John tell someone about his brother's drug problem? What can Andy do about his glue sniffing? Read on and you'll find out more about the illegal drugs you may come across at school, at parties or through your friends.

When you know the facts about drugs, decide what you would say to Adam, Emma, John and Andy.

▲ Andy sniffs glue.

# How drugs affect your body

Some illegal drugs, such as Ecstasy, cocaine and amphetamines, speed the body up. That's why they are called 'uppers'. They make people excited and alert and stop them from feeling tired. Others, like heroin, alcohol, and glue, slow the body down (downers). They make people relaxed. A few - LSD and magic mushrooms - can make people see or hear things that aren't really there (hallucinogens).

The effects of a drug also depend on how much you take, and how often, how quickly it gets into the bloodstream and what you mix it with.

Drugs come in different strengths. One joint may look the same as another but some cannabis is much stronger than other types, so you need far less to get the same effect. The same goes for cocaine, heroin and other drugs. It's impossible to tell a weak type from a strong type just by looking at them. Only the person who sold them knows.

The seller's also the only one who knows what else is in the drug. Dealers usually mix heroin or cocaine powders with other things to make them go further. It may be just sugar or salt but it could be something really dangerous, like talcum powder.

◀ Some drugs make you feel unnaturally energetic.

▲ People who take drugs can lose their homes, their jobs and their families.

Uppers, downers and hallucinogens all work on the brain. They change the way messages are sent from one nerve to another. Once a drug is in the body you can't stop it working. If it gives you a bad effect there's nothing you can do to stop it. You just have to wait for all the drug to work its way out of your system.

If you start taking drugs it can be very difficult to stop. Your mind gets hooked; all you can think about is your next fix – where and when you are going to get it. Nothing else matters. If you try to stop taking drugs it takes some time for these feelings to stop. You feel desperate. You also get nasty physical withdrawal symptoms, like cramps and fever.

It's easier to go on taking drugs, but with each fix, it gets harder and harder to stop.

# Where do drugs come from?

Some illegal drugs, such as cocaine and cannabis, come from plants. Others, like LSD and Ecstasy, are made illegally anywhere that producers can set up the equipment.

Heroin is made from morphine which comes from the opium poppy. All across South-East Asia in countries such as Afghanistan and Thailand, there are vast fields of opium poppies. The opium is harvested, the morphine extracted and turned into heroin.

▲ Growing cannabis is illegal.

The white powder is purified and transported in bulk illegally to all the major cities of the world – London, Paris, New York, Rio de Janeiro, Johannesburg, Sydney. There, it is sold to dealers who mix the pure heroin with other powders or drugs. This is partly to make more money for themselves and partly because injecting pure heroin could be fatal. It is just too powerful for the body to cope with.

◀ Opium is collected from poppy flowers. It comes out as a liquid and hardens into little balls.

Cocaine is also a white powder which is made from the leaves of the Andean coca shrub. Just as Asia is home to vast poppy fields, so vast areas of land in Peru and other parts of South America are used for growing coca. Again, the leaves are harvested and the cocaine extracted and transported all over the world.

Cannabis plants can grow almost anywhere - some users even grow them in their gardens. But large amounts are grown in Africa and Caribbean countries.

Magic mushrooms grow wild in many parts of Britain and it is not illegal to pick and eat them raw. It becomes illegal if you cook or prepare them for use as hallucinogenic drugs. The Liberty Cap is the most well known of the so-called 'magic mushrooms' but they look very like some types of poisonous mushrooms which are very dangerous.

It's hard to tell which mushrooms ▶ are hallucinogenic and which are poisonous.

Growing the plants that drugs come from causes a lot of damage to the environment. Huge areas of forestland in South America have to be slashed and burned to make room for fields of coca plants. Local people are pushed into growing drug crops instead of food. Thousands of gallons of toxic chemicals are pumped into rivers from factories where drugs are purified.

Animals and birds are poisoned and die a slow, painful death - just so that people thousands of miles away can get a buzz from their drugs.

# But my parents smoke and drink...

It's true that nicotine and alcohol are drugs as well - and millions of people use them legally every day. But they can be as dangerous as illegal drugs. Over 100,000 people die each year in Britain from heart disease, lung cancer and other nasty illnesses caused by smoking. About 70 per cent of murders, stabbings and beatings happen when people have been drinking.

▼ These young people care about the environment but they pollute it by smoking.

Other people can get hurt too. Living or working in smoky rooms can give you lung problems, such as asthma and bronchitis, even if you don't smoke. Women who smoke when they are pregnant give birth to small babies that tend to be sickly.

Alcohol causes many road accidents. Even if they aren't drunk, people who have been drinking have slower reactions. They aren't as quick to brake or swerve if a child runs out in front of them.

WE'RE TALKING ABOUT DRUGS

▲ Cigarettes are bad for smokers and for people around them who have to breathe their smoke.

Smoking is physically as well as mentally addictive. The smoker's body craves the nicotine in tobacco but it is the sticky black tar and carbon monoxide in cigarette smoke which damage the lungs, the arteries and other parts of the body. Carbon monoxide is the gas which also comes out of car exhaust.

People can become physically and mentally addicted to alcohol too. They crave a drink and the relaxing effect it has on them.

They may suffer withdrawal symptoms if they do not keep their blood topped up with alcohol. Too much alcohol damages the brain and the liver.

In Britain, it is illegal to buy or drink alcohol in bars below the age of 18, though, in Scotland, 16 and 17 year olds can buy and drink alcohol with a meal. It is also illegal to sell cigarettes to children under 16.

If you start smoking or you drink a lot it is very hard to stop. It is much easier not to get addicted in the first place.

▲ Smoking isn't grown-up and it's very bad for your body. Don't let friends persuade you to try it.

WE'RE TALKING ABOUT DRUGS

# Adam's story

Adam decided to try a joint the next time Kevin offered him one. He was sick all over his clothes and he had to tell his Mum he had food poisoning. He tried it again the following week; he wasn't sick this time but he felt very weird and it scared him. Next time Kevin offers him some cannabis he's going to say no.

▼ Smoking cannabis made Adam feel awful.

People can respond very differently to cannabis. One person may feel relaxed, happy and talkative, while another feels anxious and frightened. Cannabis isn't addictive but people who use it a lot may feel they cannot do without it.

Like alcohol, cannabis slows you down. Most people smoke it but it can also be mixed with food or drink. It works very quickly, within a few minutes.

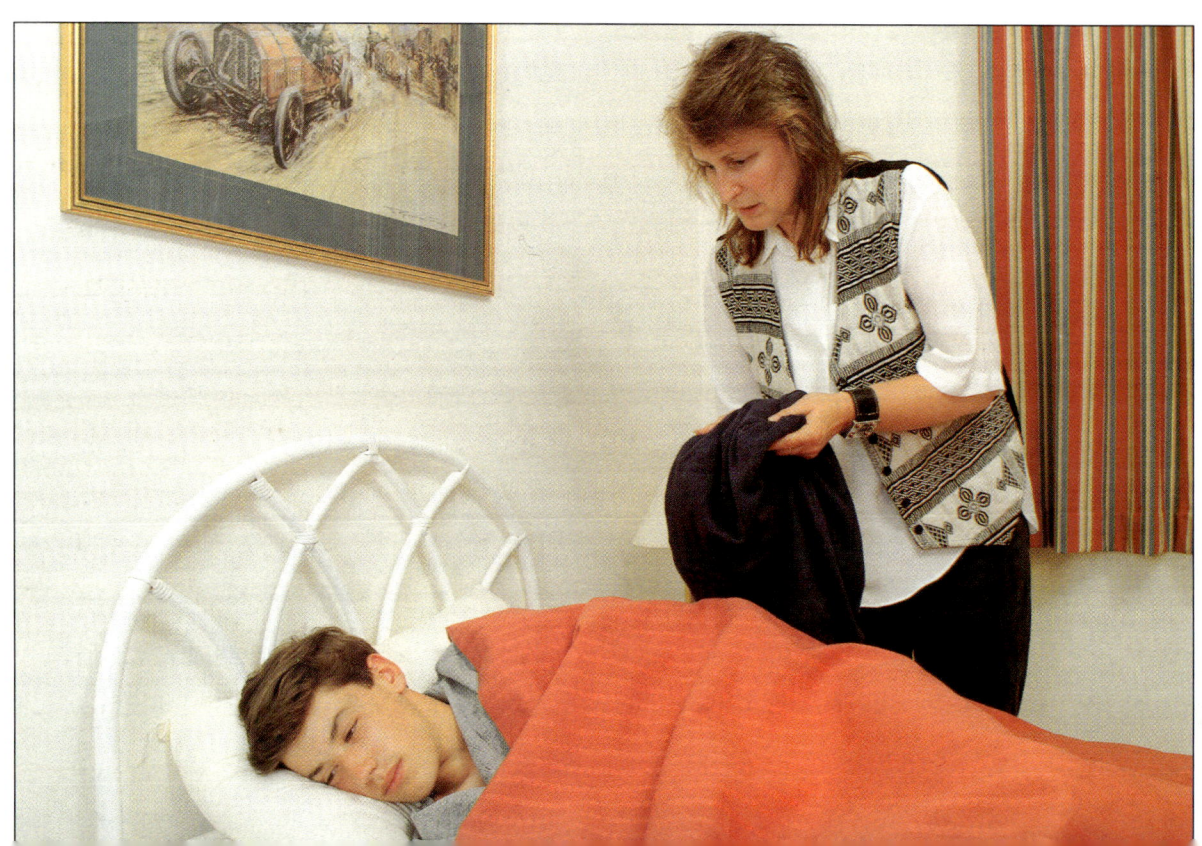

WE'RE TALKING ABOUT DRUGS

Some people are campaigning for ▶ cannabis to be legalized.

You can't think as quickly and you forget what you're doing. It is dangerous to drive a car or motorbike after taking cannabis.

It is illegal to have any cannabis or to sell it. But some people, including policemen, think it should be legalized. So many people use it that it is hard to prosecute everyone. Thirty years ago, around 2,000 people a year in the UK were found guilty of having cannabis; in the early 1990s, that figure had gone up to over 40,000.

People who are caught with cannabis now do not get in as much trouble with the law as they used to. The first time they are caught they may only get a caution and not be sent to court and fined. People who sell cannabis get into more trouble and may be sent to prison.

Cannabis is less dangerous than some other drugs, like heroin and cocaine. Experts used to worry that people who smoked cannabis might go on to take more dangerous drugs. It's true that some people do move on to heroin after cannabis but some people start on heroin without ever having used cannabis.

Like tobacco, cannabis can damage your health; the smoke contains tar and other chemicals which hurt your lungs. If, like Adam, you are offered cannabis, you need to think very carefully about whether you want to use it.

# Emma's story

At first, Emma had a really good time at the rave. Some of her friends had taken Ecstasy but she managed to avoid it. It was very hot and the music was very loud. Emma sat down because she was tired but those who had taken Ecstasy went on dancing.

Then Helen, the girl who had brought the drug to the party, collapsed on to the ground.

Someone called an ambulance and Emma went with her to the hospital. Helen was unconscious and seemed to be burning up. At the hospital, they put her on a drip and tried to cool her down. But she was unconscious and extremely ill for three days.

▼ Ecstasy makes you feel unnaturally energetic, but you feel very tired and depressed when it wears off.

Ecstasy gives people a buzz and makes them full of energy. They do not need sleep and, if they're at a party, they feel they can dance all night without stopping. Some people get away with it. After a weekend partying they sleep it off and have no lasting effects.

But there are risks. Two Ecstasy tablets may look the same but one may have three or four times the amount of drug that is in the other. You can't tell. If you take too much, or your body is very sensitive to the drug, your temperature will rise dramatically. It can go up by five or more degrees centigrade.

If you are excited and dancing you won't notice that you are getting dehydrated. This is really bad for you. The heat and lack of water in your body can damage your brain, your kidneys, your liver and other parts of your body. This can kill you.

Even people who don't collapse like Helen, can become depressed and miserable after taking Ecstasy.

▲ Ecstasy made Emma's friend very ill.

They may hallucinate and that's very frightening. If they keep taking it, they need bigger and bigger doses to get the same buzz.

Like heroin, Ecstasy can take over their lives. They don't want to do anything else. They neglect schoolwork, hobbies, family, and friends. They start to look a mess. In the end, Ecstasy changes the balance of chemicals in the brain and makes people very depressed.

If you know someone like this, try to get them to see a doctor.

WE'RE TALKING ABOUT DRUGS

# Wasted lives

US tennis star Jennifer Capriati was a victim of drugs. Her sad face was in all the newspapers. Her photograph was taken at a police station and she now has a police file for possessing cannabis. Her tennis career was put in danger because of this.

Young actor, River Phoenix, will make no more films. He died as a result of taking drugs. So did rock legends, Jimi Hendrix and Jim Morrison.

During each Olympic Games and World Cup, top sportspeople are sent home in disgrace for taking banned drugs – usually anabolic steroids. A few years ago it was sprinter Ben Johnson and footballer, Diego Maradonna.

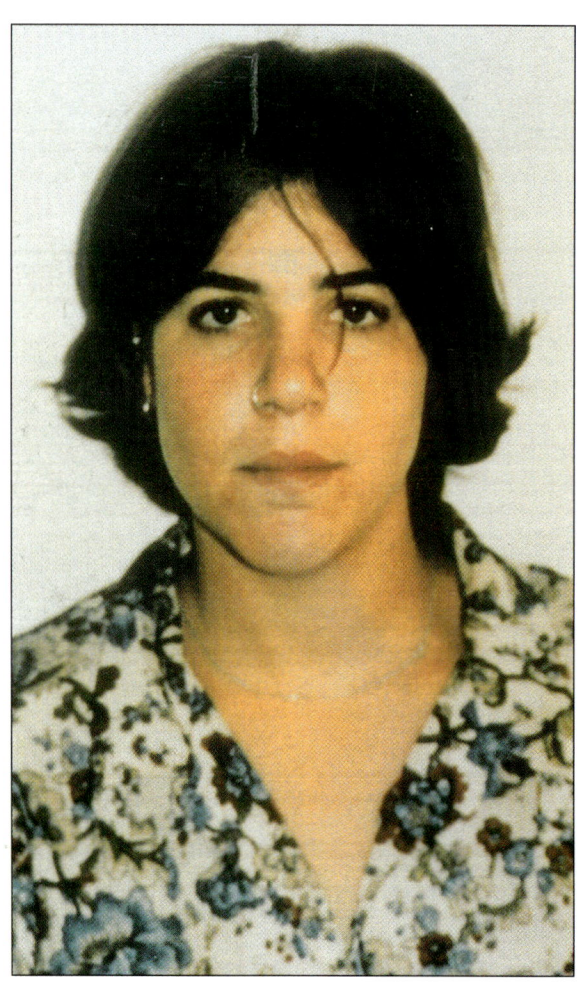

◀ Jennifer Capriati's career was endangered because of drugs.

WE'RE TALKING ABOUT DRUGS

▲ It's too late for the young actor, River Phoenix. Drugs took his life.

But often they lose their jobs and their homes, fail exams or drop out of college, and they hurt their families.

Why do they do it? There are lots of reasons why people take drugs. They are unhappy with life. Their friends take drugs. They just want to try something new. They are bored. Whatever the reason, rich or poor, the results can be just as tragic.

Anabolic steroids build muscle and athletes believe they help them train harder and recover more quickly from injury. But, in young people, they can actually stunt growth.

Thousands of young people waste their lives with drugs. Some, like Jennifer Capriati and River Phoenix, are very famous and so they make headlines. Most of the others are less well known.

▲ Kurt Cobain from the band Nirvana. Was his suicide the result of drugs?

WE'RE TALKING ABOUT DRUGS

# Richard's story

Richard didn't stop using cocaine even though John begged him to. He started to hallucinate. He was convinced that people were talking about him behind his back and even following him. His work suffered and his boss realized there was something wrong. He told him that if things did not improve Richard would be sacked.

John decided to tell his parents what was happening to Richard. They were very upset, but they weren't angry with Richard. They went to see him at his flat. At first he denied there was a problem but then he agreed he needed help.

▼ John did the right thing when he told his mum about Richard's drug problem.

▲ During group therapy, young people discuss the problems that led them to take drugs.

First, he went to his doctor. She told Richard about a local day centre where he could go for advice and counselling. Most towns have one. All the family went to talk to a counsellor specially trained in helping young people with a drug problem. The treatment was free.

Richard's parents also got in touch with a support group for families of people with a drug problem. They met other families in the same situation. They felt much better when they had talked things over and found out how other people were coping.

Some families had children who were going to hospital for treatment. They were mainly hooked on heroin and needed special help getting off their drugs. Other families had children staying at special centres for people with long term drug problems. They spent several months there.

As you can see, there are lots of different ways to help people with a drug problem – most of them free. All you need to do is ask for some help.

# Uppers and downers

Exam time is very stressful. Revision always gets left until the last minute. You stay up all night frantically trying to cram some facts into your brain and then you need to concentrate all day while you sit the papers. Then you have to start all over again, revising for tomorrow's exams. There's no time for sleep.

It's very tempting to use drugs to get you through exam time. Amphetamines – also called speed – are synthetic drugs that come in tablets, capsules or powders. They give you extra energy and make you feel more confident. You won't need to sleep and you won't want to eat either. But keep taking them and your body will start to rebel against the unnatural time clock. You may start hallucinating and feeling persecuted and, before long, you'll just collapse with exhaustion.

Don't take drugs to get you ▶ through your revision.

An even worse way to get yourself through your exams is to take amphetamines to get you through the revision and then sleeping pills or tranquillisers to bring you down between exams. Now, your body will get completely screwed up. It won't know whether it's supposed to be alert or asleep.

▲ Exam time is always stressful but everyone's in the same boat.

Within a few weeks you can become addicted to this spiral of uppers and downers and it's very hard to stop. Stopping tranquillisers causes withdrawal symptoms – people get panicky and frightened. So they stay on them and become more and more zombie-like.

No one finds exam time easy but uppers and downers won't help. It's best to have a well-organized revision programme that starts weeks before the exams – but, of course, we never do. So, when it comes to late night revision, be realistic with yourself. Set a time to stop which gives you enough sleep so you can remember what you have learned and get through the exams the next day. Staying up all night isn't the answer – you'll be so confused by morning that you won't remember half of what you have read.

# Drugs and crime

It costs an average £300 a week in Britain for addicts to pay for drugs to inject – even more if they use cocaine a lot. That's a lot of money and most people who take drugs regularly cannot work. The only way to get money for their drugs is to steal, deal in drugs, or work as prostitutes.

▼ Drug dealers do business on the 'Pill Bridge' in Amsterdam, Holland.

Drug taking and crime go together. It may start with shoplifting or pick-pocketing for a few pounds but many addicts quickly find themselves drawn into more serious crime – burglary, robbery, threats and violence. Some terrorist groups use money from selling drugs to buy guns and bombs which kill and maim innocent people.

▲ Police take a drug suspect into custody.

Once you're in that kind of world, it's very hard to get out. The people you live and mix with are very likely to be doing the same things as you.

Getting involved with drug dealers is even more dangerous. It may start with running errands in return for drugs but there are very severe penalties.

Never be tempted to carry drugs around the world — even if you are offered a lot of money. Dozens of European and American young people are suffering in rat-infested prisons in Thailand, Malaysia and other countries in the Far East after being caught with drugs. Some face the death sentence or many years living in the most squalid conditions.

The 'red light' areas of all big cities are packed with men and women who are selling their bodies to pay for their drugs — sometimes for as little as a few pounds to pay for their next fix. They may catch infections from their clients or get beaten up by them. A few of the most unlucky ones are murdered. This is the most terrifying end of the drug business — and not one that the occasional drug user is likely to come across.

But it's what can happen if drugs take over your life.

# Drugs and disease

People who take drugs are usually pretty unhealthy. You can't expect to sit in a druggy haze in the evening and work out in the gym the next morning. You only have to look at the old-before-their-time faces of pop stars of the 60s and 70s who used drugs to see the long term effects.

▼ Heroin addiction isn't pretty. Can you see the puncture marks on this woman's arm?

But you don't have to wait as long as thirty years to be ill. People who have had bad experiences with LSD or magic mushrooms can go on having flashbacks and hallucinations for months or even years afterwards. Many of those who take Ecstasy or cocaine become depressed and even suicidal as it becomes harder and harder to get a buzz from their drugs.

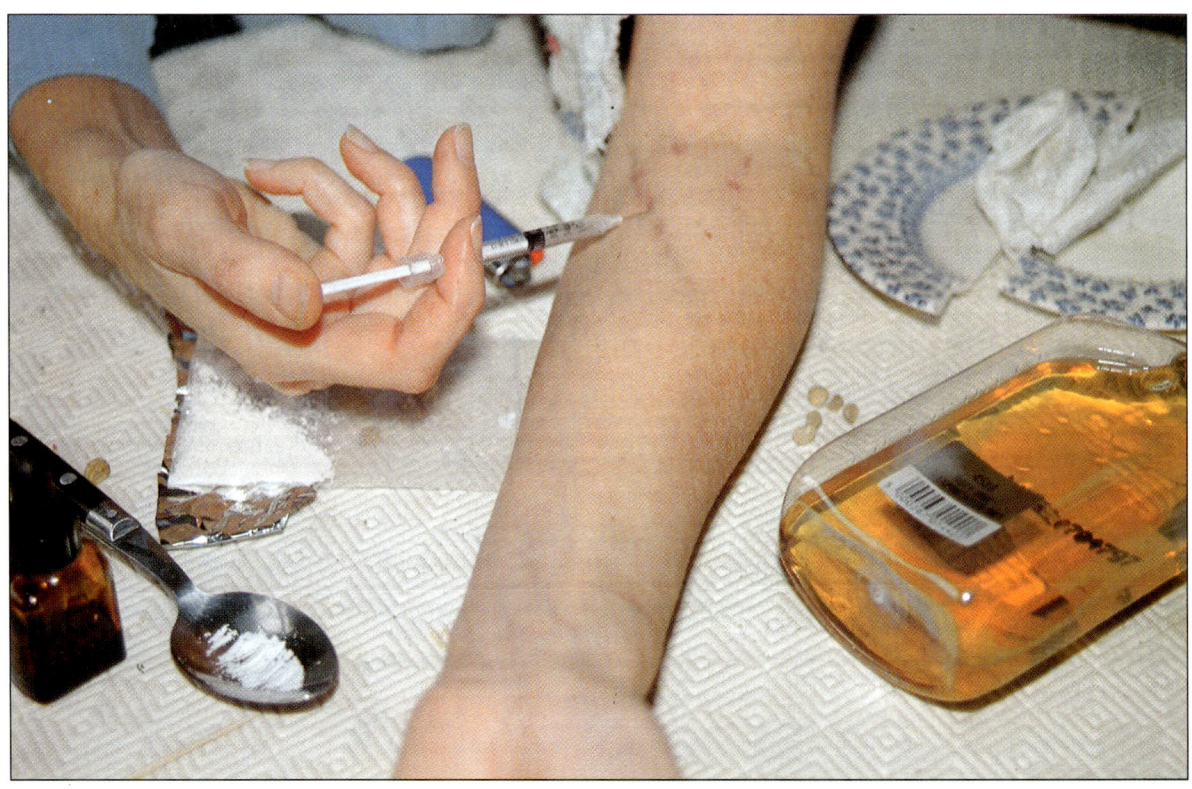

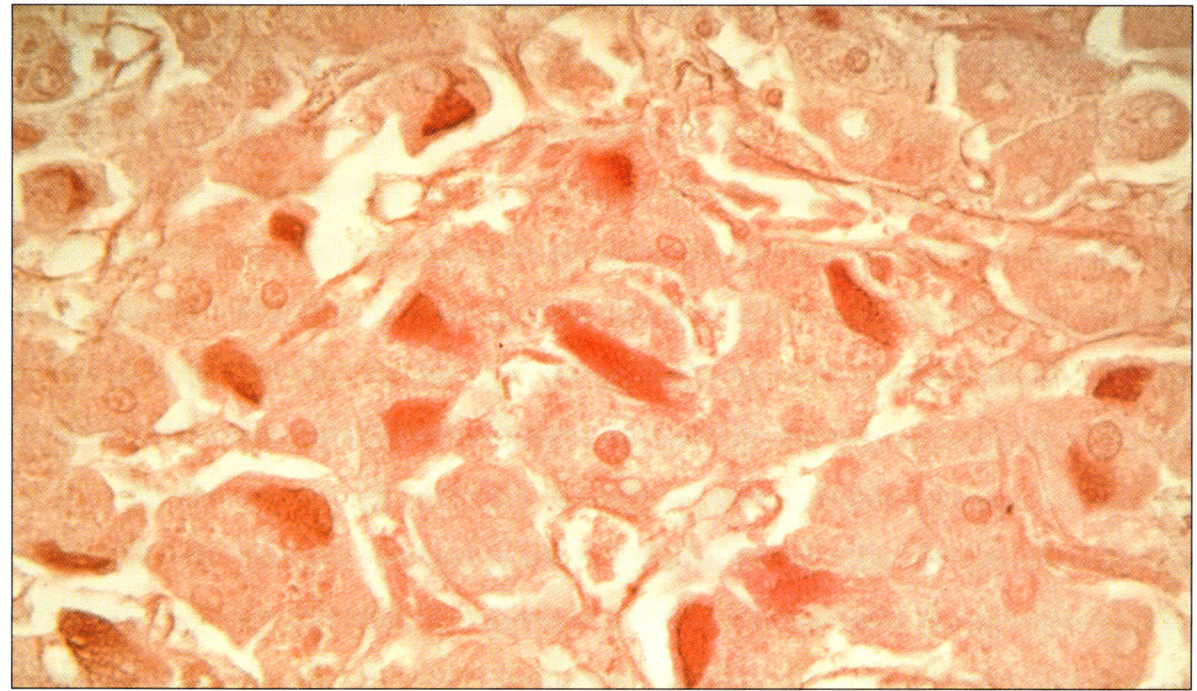

▲ This microscope photograph shows a human liver infected with hepatitis.

Injecting drugs carries even greater health hazards, especially if the addict shares needles or other equipment with another user. Some people who inject drugs carry the viruses which cause hepatitis B or AIDS, sometimes both. Hepatitis B can be fatal and AIDS always kills you in the end.

The hepatitis B virus attacks the liver. There is no cure and it takes months of hospital treatment to get better. Some people don't. Others are left with liver damage.

AIDS is caused by the human immunodeficiency virus (HIV) which attacks the immune system. Victims can no longer defend themselves from infections. They get sicker and sicker and eventually die.

Both hepatitis B and HIV are passed between people in blood and other body fluids. People who share needles when injecting heroin inevitably pass on small amounts of their blood.

# Andy's story

Sniffing glue may sound pretty harmless after reading about the horrors of hard drugs, like heroin and cocaine, but solvents kill nearly as many people as heroin. Each year, in Britain, about 150 young people die using solvents. Squirting gas or aerosols straight down the throat is especially dangerous and can kill instantly.

Andy was secretly rather glad when his parents found out about his glue sniffing. It was making him ill but he didn't know how to stop. His parents were shocked and sad but they weren't angry. They talked to him about his problem and took him to see a drugs counsellor. Nobody told the police or any of Andy's teachers and he didn't get into trouble.

Andy told his glue sniffing friends he didn't want to do it any more. Some of them wouldn't speak to him any more but two of them agreed with Andy and the three of them found other things to do after school and at weekends. They joined a youth club which arranged trips and organized a football team. There were discos on Fridays and Andy made more friends.

◀ In Britain, about 150 young people die each year from solvent abuse.

Andy's father managed to find more time to do things with him. Sometimes they went swimming, other times they just kicked a ball about on the local playing fields.

▲ Andy has found much better things to do instead of glue sniffing.

Andy often saw the old glue sniffing gang. They just hung about town, doing the same boring old things.

# Getting help

There are lots of places where you can get help for a drug problem. The best thing is to ask your parents for help. If you do not feel you can do that, perhaps you could talk to your teacher. If you are really scared, ring the Samaritans. They are not just for people who want to kill themselves. The number for your local branch is in the phonebook.

There is also a free helpline available just for drug-related problems – phone the National Drugs Helpline on 0800 776600. Or you can phone Release on 0171 729 9904 Monday to Friday, 10a.m.–6p.m., or 0171 603 8654 at other times).

▼ Drug addicts at a Rehabilitation Centre discuss their problems with family and friends.

There are many helpful booklets and leaflets on drug and solvent problems. You can get some at your local library or from the Institute for the Study of Drug Dependence, Waterbridge House, 32–36 Loman Street, London SE1 0EE. Tel: 0171 928 1211.

For problems with glue and solvents, you can contact Re-Solv, 30A High Street, Stone, Staffordshire, ST15 8AW. Tel: 01785 817885.

Also outside London, are Lifeline in Manchester, telephone 0161 839 2054, and the Mersey Drug Information Centre in Liverpool, Tel: 0151 709 3511. In Scotland, contact Scottish Drugs Forum, 5 Oswald Street, Glasgow G1 4QR. Tel: 0141-221-1175.

There are two organizations for families and friends of people with drug problems: ADFAM provides a national helpline on 0171 405 3923 and Families Anonymous is a self-help group for parents of users, with branches all over the country. Tel: 0171 498 4680.

▲ There are various helplines you can ring for confidential advice about drug related problems.

# Glossary

**Amphetamines** are also called speed, uppers, sulphate, sulph, whiz, Berwick.

**Barbiturates** are also called barbs, blues, reds, sekkies.

**Cannabis** is also called dope, blow, wacky backy, grass, shit, puff, draw, smoke.

**Cocaine** is also called snow, crack base, Charlie, C, coke.

**Crack cocaine** is cheaper but more dangerous than cocaine. It's sometimes called rock. It is cocaine that has been treated with chemicals so that it can be smoked. The 'high' people get is followed by unpleasant after-effects which can lead to dependence.

**Ecstasy** is also called 'E', dennis the menace, rhubarb and custard, new yorkers, love doves, disco burgers and phase 4.

**Heroin** is also called smack, junk, H, skag, gear.

**LSD** is also called acid, blotter, flash, Lucy, trips.

**Tranquillisers** are also called tranx, benzos, eggs, jellies, Temazies.

# Further reading

*Drugs and Solvents: A Young Person's Guide,* a free leaflet from your library (DSS, 1992)

*Drugs and Solvents: Things You Should Know,* a free leaflet from your library (DSS, 1993)

*Drug Warning* by David Stockley (Little Brown, 1992)

*Living with Drugs* by Michael Gossop (Ashgate, 1993)

**For older readers:**

*Face the Facts: Drugs* by Adrian King (Wayland, 1997)

*What do you know about Drugs?* by Pete Saunders and Steve Myers (Watts, 1995)

**For parents:**

*Drugs: A Parent's Guide,* a free leaflet from your library (DSS, 1992)

*Drugs and Solvents: You and Your Child,* a free leaflet from your library (DSS, 1993)

*Solvents: A Parent's Guide,* a free leaflet from your library (DSS, 1993)

# Index

addiction  11, 12, 21
aerosols  26
AIDS 25
alcohol 6, 10, 12
amphetamines 6, 20
annabolic steroids 16, 17

cannabis 4, 6, 8, 9, 12-13
cigarettes 4
cocaine  5, 6, 8, 9, 18, 22, 24, 26
counselling 19
crime  22

dealers  6, 8, 23
dehydration  15
depression  15, 24
doctors  15, 19
downers  6, 7, 21

Ecstasy  4, 6, 8, 14, 15, 24
environment, damage to 9
exams 20

glue  5, 6, 26-7

hallucinogens  6, 7, 9, 15, 18, 20, 24

kidneys 15

LSD  6, 8, 24

magic mushrooms 6, 9, 24
morphine  8

nicotine  10

opium poppy  8

prison  13, 23
prostitutes  22

raves 4, 14

Samaritans 28
solvents 26
speed 20
support groups 19

tranquillisers 21

uppers  6, 7, 21

withdrawal symptoms  7, 11